LEARNING QUESTS
FOR GIFTED PUPILS

BOOK 3

AGES 6-9

DEBBIE SMITH

Scaffolding into cross-curricular studies

Title:	Learning Quests for Gifted Pupils. Book 3 – Ages 6-9
Author:	Debbie Smith
Editor:	Paula Wagemaker
Design:	Delineate Limited
Book Code:	PB00131
ISBN:	978-1-908736-10-9
Published:	2012
Publisher:	TTS Group Ltd
	Park Lane Business Park Kirkby-in-Ashfield Notts, NG17 9GU Tel: 0800 318 686 Fax: 0800 137 525
Website:	www.tts-shopping.com
Copyright:	Text © Debbie Smith, 2008 Edition and illustrations: © TTS Group Ltd, 2012
About the author:	Debbie Smith is a New Zealand-trained and registered teacher with an interest in gifted and talented education, educational technologies, and special needs. She has written articles for magazines and journals, with the aim of sharing her passion and ideas about gifted education and using educational technologies. Debbie is intent on being "an extra pair of hands" for dedicated teachers trying to understand the unique needs of gifted and talented pupils. As well as this series of books, Debbie has written www.thinkers.co.nz, a website that provides tools for teachers and gifted pupils. This site assists teachers to differentiate their lessons, thereby helping make school a more welcoming place for gifted pupils. Readers are welcome to email her at info@debbie.co.nz.

Photocopy Notice:

Permission is given to schools and teachers who buy this book to reproduce it (and/or any extracts) by photocopying or otherwise, but only for use at their present school. Copies may not be supplied to anyone else or made or used for any other purpose.

Contents

Introduction	4
Presentation and Use of the Learning *Quests*	5
Unit Assessment	7

Units

One: A Community of Learners — 8
Teacher Notes — 8
1.1 Working as a Community — 9
1.2 The Ants and the Bees — 13

Two: So Many Questions — 17
Teacher Notes — 17
2.1 Review Questions and Answers — 18
2.2 Good Questions to Investigate — 22

Three: Personal Space — 26
Teacher Notes — 26
3.1 Give Me Space — 27
3.2 Bursting Your Bubble — 31

Four: Tenacity and Compromise — 35
Teacher Notes — 35
4.1 The Tortoise and the Hare — 36
4.2 Helen Keller — 40

Five: Overcoming Frustration — 44
Teacher Notes — 44
5.1 Getting Started — 45
5.2 Hieroglyphics — 49

Suggested Answers for Specified Activities — 53

Introduction

The first book written in this series focused on helping teachers get to know the gifted children in their classrooms by offering them Quick, Unique, Educationally Satisfying Tasks (**Quests**). The tasks (set under thematic units of work) allowed younger pupils to practise working independently and therefore used a simpler format than the ones used in the **Learning *Quests*** for Key Stages 2 and 3. The first book also gave teachers a chance to explore, through some fairly open-ended activities, the ways gifted children think. As I wrote at the time, the units would do nothing except create busy work for the gifted child unless the teacher also read and discussed the activities with the pupils, in order to find out the reasons behind some of these children's answers. I wish to re-emphasise this point at the outset of this book.

When gifted pupils first enter school, after a possibly very stimulating one-on-one preschool environment, they often find the transition very rocky. Class structure and content can challenge what they believe school is supposed to be. Their endless supply of questions can interfere with the normal flow of classroom life, and frustrate all concerned. Suddenly, the gifted child doesn't have his or her questions answered as immediately, the other pupils lose interest in the examples and discussion of the highly able pupil, and the teacher has to become a master juggler.

The pressure may have come off the parent between 9 and 3 each day, but it certainly goes onto the teacher and the rest of the class. It is important not only to recognise that integrating gifted children's needs into the classroom task is necessary, but also to appreciate the complexity of doing so in a mainstream classroom. Often, teachers are doing their best in a group environment not originally designed to meet pupils' one-on-one needs.

Schools and teachers are being asked to do more and more to meet children's diverse needs, but the reality, as you will know, is that often you need more than one pair of hands and eyes and ears to do it! You have to try to balance the needs of an intense discussion on the mat for the gifted child, with the shorter attention spans and understanding levels of other pupils. It is considerations such as these that make working as a partner with the children and their parents absolutely necessary.

You will also find that being realistic about parental expectations is a must, but so is listening to and understanding what parents are telling you about their child. Some of the unique traits associated with gifted children can be contrary to the working habits you are trying to develop in your classroom. Sometimes a compromise is needed for all to cope with the gifted child's needs within the dynamics of a regular classroom.

Presentation and Use of the Learning *Quests*

This book has progressed from the original format used for the **Quests** in the first book to one in which each unit is based on one common characteristic of gifted children and includes a teacher page and two sub-units for each topic.

- **Teacher Page:** This provides you with an informative introduction to the characteristics commonly found in gifted pupils. My aim in first teaching you, the teacher, is that you will gain a more understanding attitude or acceptance of these pupils. We need to see that some of their traits are not just a matter of the gifted child being "naughty". Far too often, gifted children are with-held from programmes because of behavioural issues, which would likely diminish if they were in a programme that better suited their needs. The teacher page is probably the most important page of each unit, because if we do not grasp an understanding of these basic characteristics, we may never know the needs of the gifted children that we are trying to meet.

- **Sub-units:** Each unit is divided into two sub-units. These, in turn, are divided into the following four stages:

1. **Pre–*Quest*: The Story So Far …**
   This is where the gifted characteristic is defined and introduced to the pupil, generally by way of a well-known story or an activity that has similar vocabulary or represents the trait involved. This step can offer a "recording place" within which your gifted children tell you more about themselves and the way they learn. If there are discrepancies in this respect, please ask the children to explain what they mean. Their reasons will give you good insights into their thinking processes.

2. **In–*Quest*: I Understand …** These activities show how the facts of the story are reflected in the trait being discussed. They allow you to check that the pupils have thought about what they have been reading or discussing before they are asked to use their knowledge in creative ways. The activities also let you make sure that the pupils haven't done a cursory read, but that they actually understand what is being discussed. By asking deeper-level questions, the activities furthermore allow you to gain an even deeper appreciation of the pupils' level of understanding. You will find that some of the activities in this part of the unit also draw on analogies or abstract thinking.

3. ***Quest*–ion: What If I … ?** "What if …" scenarios encourage gifted pupils to think outside the square. At this stage, pupils will also start to explore alternative realities or possible solutions to the problems that have been identified. This approach helps the children understand they have the power to make positive changes rather than just accept a situation as it stands. Exploring problems from characters in literature and then seeing those same problems in similar real-life situations can be an empowering experience. Gifted pupils prefer to deal with real-world problems, but they sometimes need us to bridge the gaps for them. This stage of the unit also gives you and your pupils a chance to explore their creativity.

4. **Con–*Quest*: Look What I've Done!** Here, pupils can proudly display what they have done or made, what conclusions they have reached, and how they propose to deal with any issues in the classroom. This step helps pupils become more aware of their own needs and how they can meet them independently. In this infant-level book, the outcomes are more guided, but if any of your gifted children are mature enough to cope with deciding their own methods of displaying what they have learned, don't be afraid to negotiate alternative forms of **Con–*Quests*** with them.

While the children can write and complete many of the activities on the A4 pages supplied, you may want to photocopy (using the enlargement facility) the task worksheets onto A3 paper, as this will make it easier for younger pupils with their generally larger handwriting style to work on the tasks. You or the pupils could staple the sheets into a large booklet as a record for you and as a means on which to base future learning activities. Alternatively, you could glue these sheets flat into a scrapbook, so the pages don't get folded in half. It seems to devalue children's work if you put a crease through the middle of it to glue it into a book that is too small. Another approach is simply to gather the sheets together in a clearfile, but your decision to do this may depend on your pupils' ability to keep things organised!

At the end of the resource (pages 53–55), you'll find answers for specified activities within each unit. Many of the answers given there are suggested answers only, to guide you with the sorts of questioning you could use if pupils get stuck while doing the work. Note, however, that gifted pupils can take quite a different meaning from what was intended, so before you steer them back onto the "right" direction, make sure you question how they came to their conclusion. Sometimes it can be a valid interpretation that we must accept. Redirecting pupils to the "right" answer will not always be taken graciously, so carefully consider how you might tackle these sensitive issues. After all, if we have communicated to them poorly, why should they have to redo the work? Well, that is what some of them will probably think, at best!

Unit Assessment

Self-Assessment

- I have completed the unit called _____.

- Draw a smiley face or a frowning face to show how you felt about ◯
  your work on this unit.

- Mark on the line how well you think you answered this unit.

_____

I could have done better   I did OK; I'm happy   I did my absolute best

- My favourite activity in this unit was _____
  _____.

- I could have improved my work by _____
  _____.

Teacher-Assessment

- Unit name _____

- Mark on the line how well you think the pupil answered this unit.

_____

It could be done better   It is OK; I'm happy   It is absolutely fantastic

- I especially liked _____
  _____.

- I would like to see more work done on _____
  _____.

- An area you have improved on is _____
  _____.

- An area that still needs improvement is _____
  _____.

© TTS Group Ltd, 2012

Unit One: A Community of Learners

Teacher Notes

"No man is an Island"—John Donne (1572–1631), an English clergyman and poet.

We all belong to a worldwide community—broken and disjointed as it might be at times. We depend on one another to varying degrees, which becomes very evident when rising oil prices start to hammer our bank accounts, for example! Various forms of self-sufficient communities are dotted across the globe, but even within them, some individuals are more skilled at doing some jobs than others. We choose to use the strengths of some people to balance out the weaknesses in others. No one person has to be absolutely excellent at every job there is to achieve recognition in the community. Just one skill can be used to trade for other goods and services required. But make sure the skill you have stays in demand!

In a class of learners, there will also be a wide variety of skills. We can all benefit from this vast skill base if we learn to be a sharing and caring community. There will be times when we might be relied upon to provide our skills for the benefit of ourselves and others, and times when others will reciprocate. This is where the gifted often start to come unstuck in the classroom community. There may be many occasions when they can assist others, but not too many times when they need (or think they need) assistance themselves. Perhaps the assistance they need cannot be provided by others, an imbalance that may become a source of frustration. How can this situation be remedied?

Firstly, some outside-the-"cube" thinking is needed. Can any specialist teachers or parents in the school community be used as "more expert others" and called on to answer some of the more pressing questions your gifted pupils ask? Maybe you could arrange for the headteacher or a parent mentor to help when needed. Email contact is quite unobtrusive, as long as questions are limited in quantity, and there is a guarantee that the recipient will answer questions within a fairly short time frame (we are talking about incessant questioners, remember). Or how about using the various question lines on internet's "Ask an Expert"? Maybe a new approach to using spelling gurus in the class would not be to send pupils to them as words are needed, but to get these whiz kids to make a more kid-friendly spelling list for use in the classroom and to operate it on the principle of "Write it once, use it many times!"

Unit 1.1

Learning *Quest*

WORKING AS A COMMUNITY

Pre-*Quest*: The Story So Far ...

Imagine you are sitting on the mat and the teacher asks a hard question, and you think you are the only one who knows the answer to it. What do you do? (Tick the box that states what you would most likely do.)

☐ You just explode with excitement and shout out the answer.

☐ You sit and wait for someone else to answer who puts their hand up first.

Shouting out the answer can upset the children who wait their turn in the class.

Tick the boxes of the *good* things you think result from shouting out:

☐ Other classmates are upset you haven't given them time to think of the answer.

☐ You have annoyed the whole class by not waiting to be asked.

☐ You have shown the teacher you were listening.

☐ You have robbed other classmates of the opportunity to come up with an answer.

☐ You have shown the teacher, yet again, how intelligent you are.

☐ You get to say your answer before you forget it.

Your teacher explains that by shouting out the answer, you have actually stolen something from someone else. Who could you possibly have stolen from?

_____

What have you stolen from them? _____

_____

_____

What other way would you describe your action of "shouting out"?

_____

_____

_____

© TTS Group Ltd, 2012

💡 In-*Quest*: I Understand

Comprehension is the word given to how well we understand the things that have been said. Often when we listen, we can confuse the meaning of what we hear, just because we come from a different background. How might the background situations below affect how we understand something? Use the examples given to explain your answers.

A. Our age can cause us to misunderstand why people wear different fashion items. We might not understand why teenagers wear …
B. Our own life experiences can stop us from understanding causes of robbery when we come from a safe community. We might not understand that we need to …
C. We might not understand if the problem is something we are not familiar with. An example might be …
D. Our home culture can affect our understanding of what immigrants do. We might not understand why …
My own example …

Whose responsibility is it to make sure the communication is understood?

☐ The speaker ☐ The listener ☐ Both responsible

💡 *Quest*-ion: What If I ... ?

In the bubbles below, write the sorts of things you would consider when problem-solving how to deal with Goldilocks if you found her asleep in your bed and you were Baby Bear!

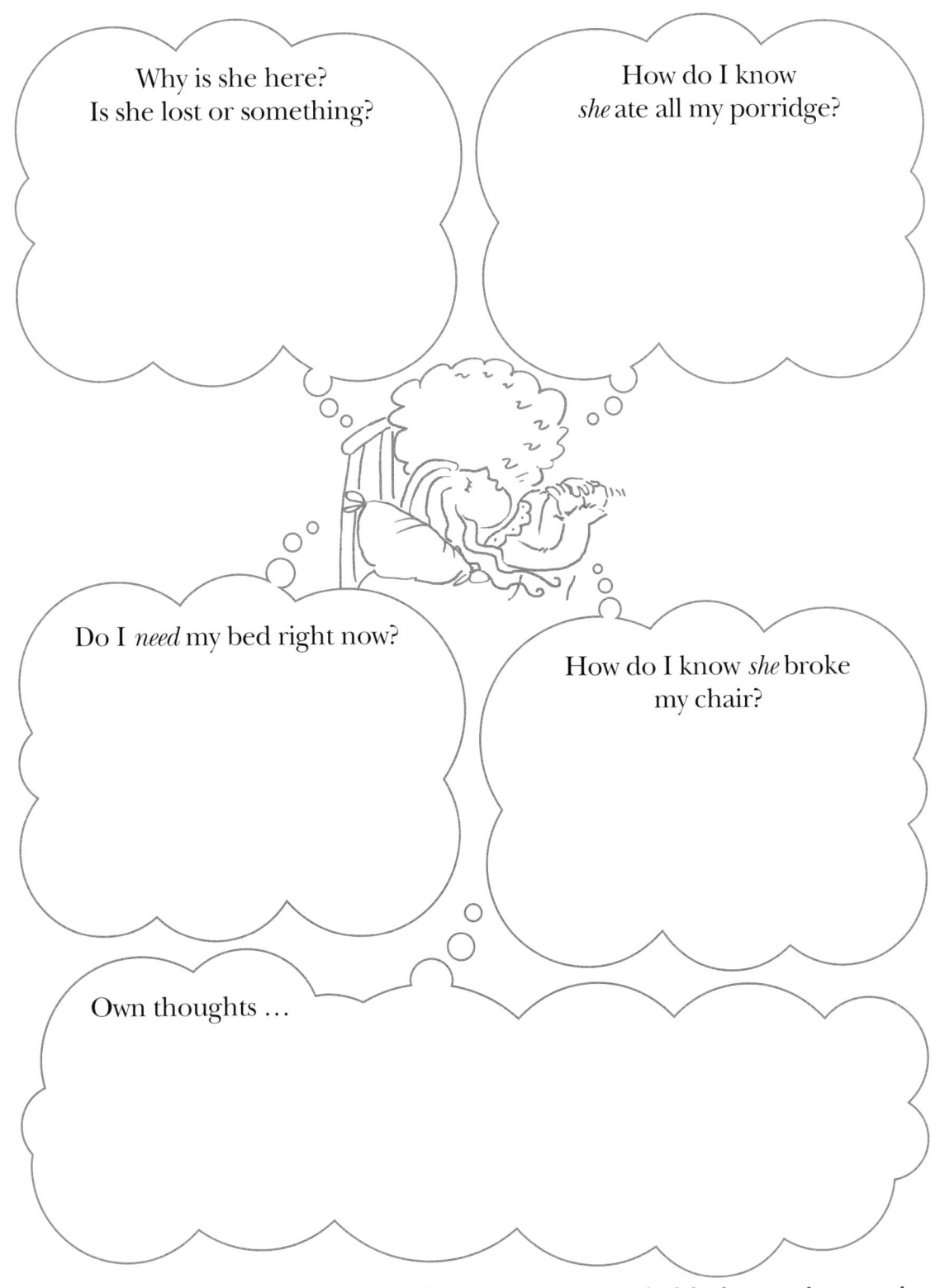

> Why is she here?
> Is she lost or something?

> How do I know *she* ate all my porridge?

> Do I *need* my bed right now?

> How do I know *she* broke my chair?

> Own thoughts ...

What do you think? Did Goldilocks run because she was scared of the bears or because she felt guilty for being there and all the damage she caused? Be ready to discuss your answer.

💡 Con-*Quest*: Look What I've Done!

Sometimes we have to find another way to communicate with our teacher to show that we know the answer, but also to give other children a chance to answer. What could you do, or what plans could you make with your teacher, so that your answer is acknowledged?

Example 1:
Thumbs up!

Example 2:
Whisper my answer to a "buddy" who has their hand up too.

Unit 1.2

Learning *Quests*

THE ANTS AND THE BEES

💡 Pre-*Quest*: The Story So Far...

Ants and honey bees are two insects that live in communities. This means they all work together doing different jobs to help everyone survive. Choose either the ant or the bee and draw and name various members of their "community"—for example, the Queen, the workers, etc. Write about each of the jobs they do in their own community.

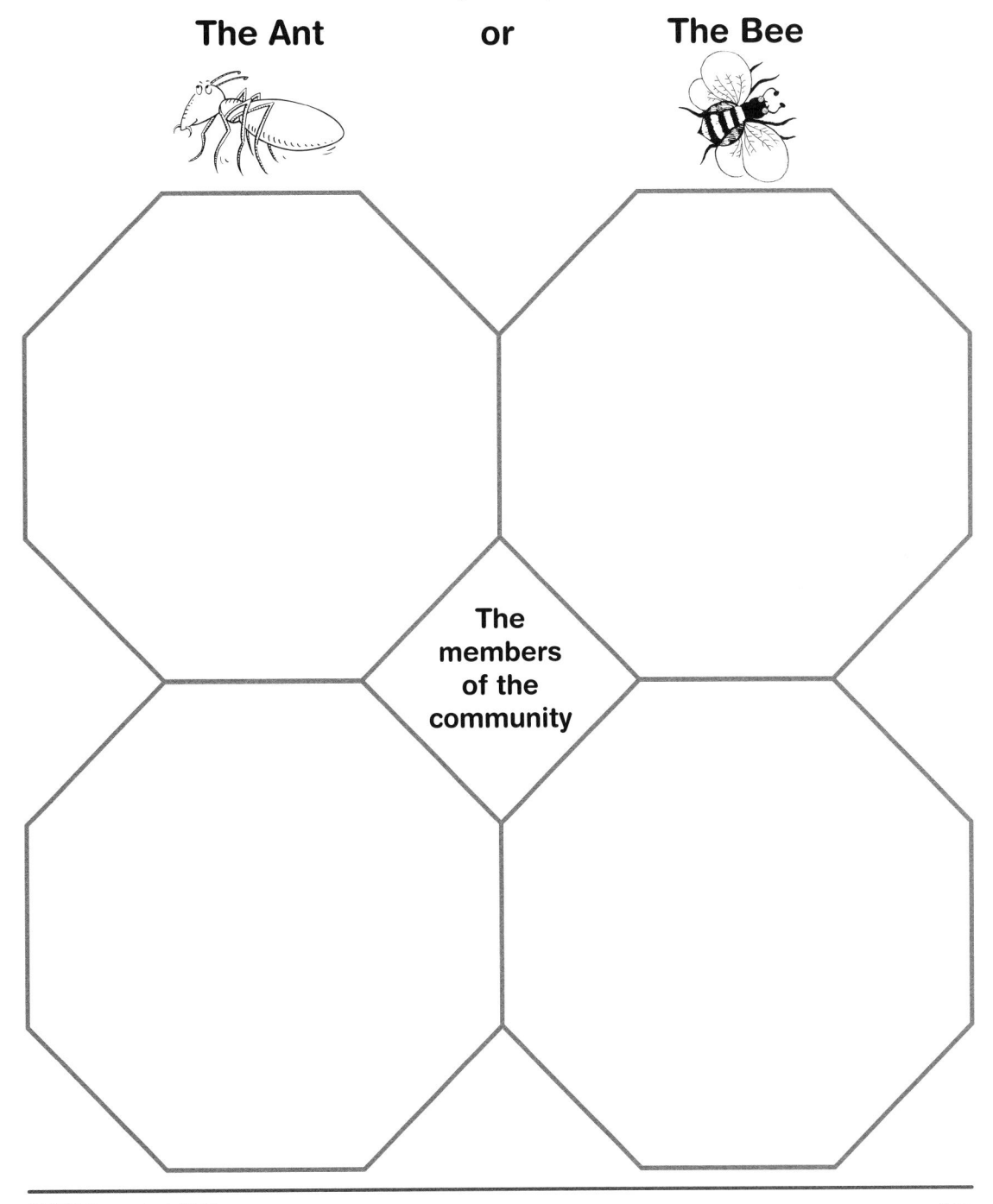

The Ant or **The Bee**

The members of the community

In-*Quest*: I Understand

People and animals often operate in communities. How do "people communities" use the same breakdown of specific jobs for their community so that it runs as well as possible? Explain, using the types of job listed below:

Workers

_____
_____
_____

Builders

_____
_____
_____

Caretakers

_____
_____
_____

Designers

_____
_____
_____

Leaders

_____
_____
_____

Think of another type of job they could do and write it here.

_____
_____
_____

💡 Quest–ion: What If I … ?

Think about how you would "advertise" yourself for a job that really suits your skills and interests.

- What are your strengths?

  _____

  _____

- What are your "passions" (those things you most like doing)?

  _____

  _____

- What do you know a lot about already?

  _____

  _____

- What sort of job do you think you would be best suited for? Tick any of the following that apply to you, and write down a couple of your own in your exercise book.

  ☐ Working with your hands?

  ☐ Thinking about things in the future?

  ☐ Sorting out problems?

  ☐ Working with other people?

  ☐ Working with your brain?

  ☐ Working by yourself?

  ☐ Working with animals?

  ☐ Discovering new things?

© TTS Group Ltd, 2012

💡 Con-*Quest*: Look What I've Done!

All sorts of different jobs are done every day in the classroom. How could we use one another's strengths as a community to help all of us learn better? From your class …

- Who could you put in a "master speller" group? _____
  _____

- Who could you put in a "creative drawing" team? _____
  _____

- Who could you put in a "creative ideas" team? _____
  _____

- Who could you put in a "proof-reading team" to check all your written work?
  _____

- Who could you put in a "master mathematicians" group? _____
  _____

- What are the benefits of sharing our strengths like this? _____
  _____
  _____

- What are the bad points about sharing our strengths like this?
  _____
  _____

- How would you feel if the "master speller" job kept you from doing your other work?
  _____
  _____

Make up some rules that would help these specialist people get their own work done. For example, if you need a token to ask for a favour, and you have to earn each token by doing a favour, then you only get help as many times as you help others.

1.
2.
3.
4.

Unit Two: So Many Questions

Teacher Notes

Parents of gifted children, right from their early childhood, are usually run ragged trying to answer all their children's questions. Why do gifted pupils ask so many questions? Or, indeed, do they ask enough?

A question is more than a comment. The questioner expects some thought given to the topic— and a response. You may ask a question to gain new information or to prompt someone else into discussing what they think about a topic. Either way, questions encourage a response. And because we want to encourage a deeper form of responsiveness in our gifted pupils, we must learn how to deal with the volume of questions, not just avoid them or—worse still—discourage them!

Some time ago when I was at a seminar, I learned the use of "carparking" questions, and ever since I have found it an excellent tool to use in the classroom. How many times do your discussions on the mat get taken off topic by those creative thinkers in the room, and the majority of the class then ending up spending too long on the mat? But instead of discouraging those comments, have a space on your whiteboard in which to record ("carpark") questions that you will deal with later. This approach prevents the askers forgetting the question when you ask them about it later, and it also tends to satisfy them long enough for you to get back on topic and keep the majority of the pupils on task. Sometimes your discussion of the carpark questions can take place one on one just as everyone is leaving the mat, or you could keep the questions for reflection time later in the day.

With gifted pupils, the types of questions you ask them should send them into a deeper form of reflection, and from there yield answers that have more impact and are less superficial. Answering a question with another question is also good for encouraging discussion. Pupils will learn there are not just right and wrong answers. If you model the use of questions to get more information, challenge viewpoints, soften a negative response, and keep on topic, your pupils soon learn to do these things too. I find it really helpful to have Bloom's Taxonomy question starters visible in the classroom so that I can get prompts for questions from the various levels of ability evident among the pupils. Basic comprehension can satisfy an average pupil, but the gifted usually want to think about things in greater depth. Asking these pupils to analyse or synthesise the facts helps stretch their minds in far more challenging ways.

Unit 2.1

Learning *Quest*

REVIEW QUESTIONS AND ANSWERS

Pre-*Quest*: The Story So Far …

What sorts of information do you get from the various questions below? Match the question stem on the left with a suitable answer on the right.

Who?	Explanation of the way something happened or is about to happen.
What?	The timing—past, present or future—to do with a set event.
Where?	Names of people and descriptions of people, or titles, such as Mr or Dr.
When?	The reason for doing something; an excuse for something that happened.
Why?	A place or a venue for something; a description of a position of something.
How?	Action of some sort; something that has happened.

In-*Quest*: I Understand

Sometimes we talk about **The BIG Question**. The big question is like the outside of an umbrella because we can break it down into many smaller questions, like the spiked segments of the umbrella.

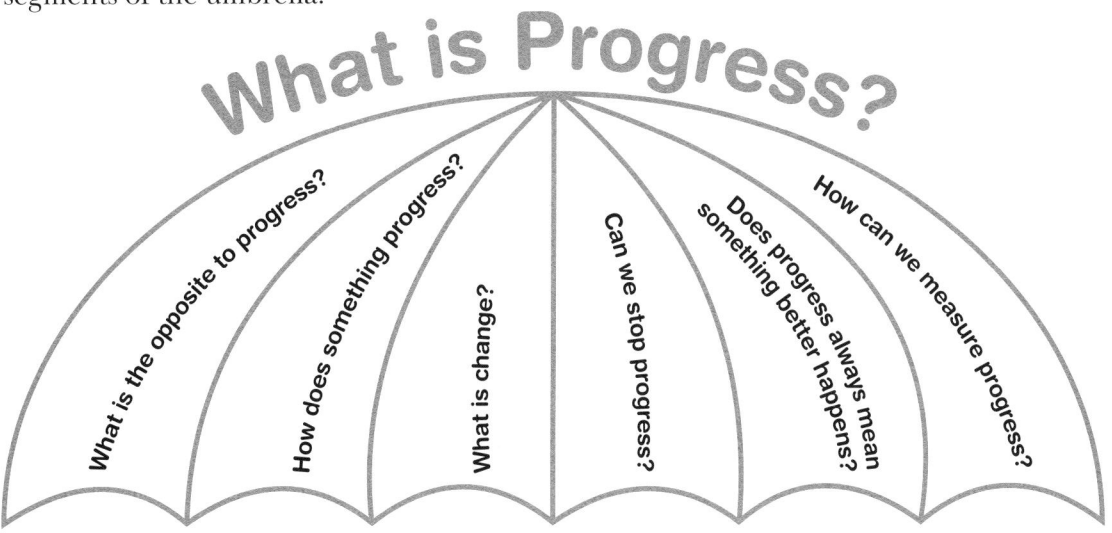

What is Progress?

- What is the opposite to progress?
- How does something progress?
- What is change?
- Can we stop progress?
- Does progress always mean something better happens?
- How can we measure progress?

It is by breaking down a big question into smaller questions that we can find out much more about a topic, and this makes us better able to answer the original big question.

Think of your own "big question". Write it on the outside of the umbrella. Here are some examples: What is the future? What is safety? What is happiness?

Now break down your big question into smaller questions on your umbrella shape, and then use your questions to find out more about your topic.

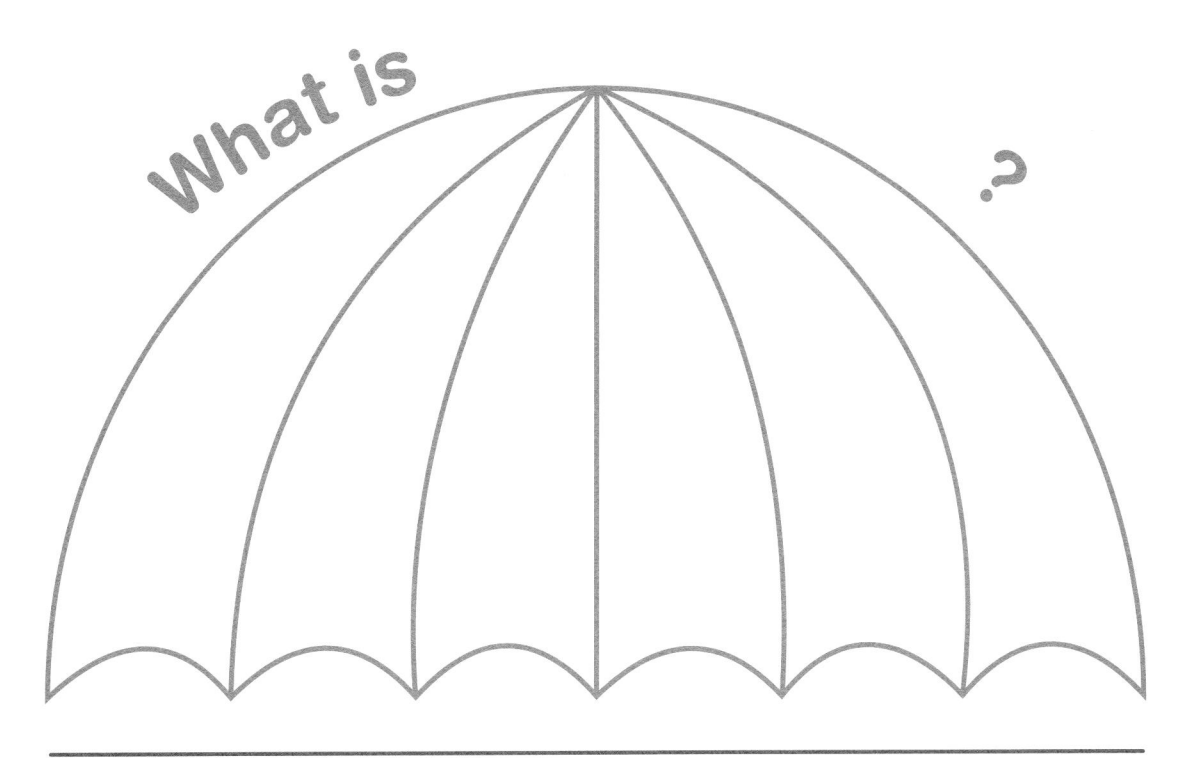

What is ____?

Quest-ion: What If I ... ?

The smaller questions should help you answer your **BIG Question**.

Example: Using the big question, "What is Wealth?" think about and fill in your responses to these smaller questions below.

A. How would things change if I were wealthier than I am now?
___
___

B. How could my wealth affect other people around me?
___
___

C. What things might I see through a different set of glasses?
___
___

D. What could I do if I were wealthy that I can't do now?
___
___

E. What might it be like if I never became wealthy?
___
___

F. What if I became wealthy and then lost all my wealth again?
___
___

G. What sort of feelings might change if I became wealthy?
___
___

H. Does wealth mean you have to have money? Or can you be wealthy in another form? If so, what?
___
___

If I was really wealthy, I would like to …
___
___

Con–*Quest*: Look What I've Done!
How to present the findings from your BIG Question ...

When we consider a big question, we can end up with a very large answer that covers all the different areas relating to that question. But we can make the answer clearer by answering the question in short, well-thought out sentences, and perhaps presenting the information as a poster. Big questions are really all about getting people to think outside the square.

Make a poster that helps explain to others all the issues involved in your big question. Make it stand out by employing good use of space and colour, writing short, clear statements, and having an overall eye-catching design.

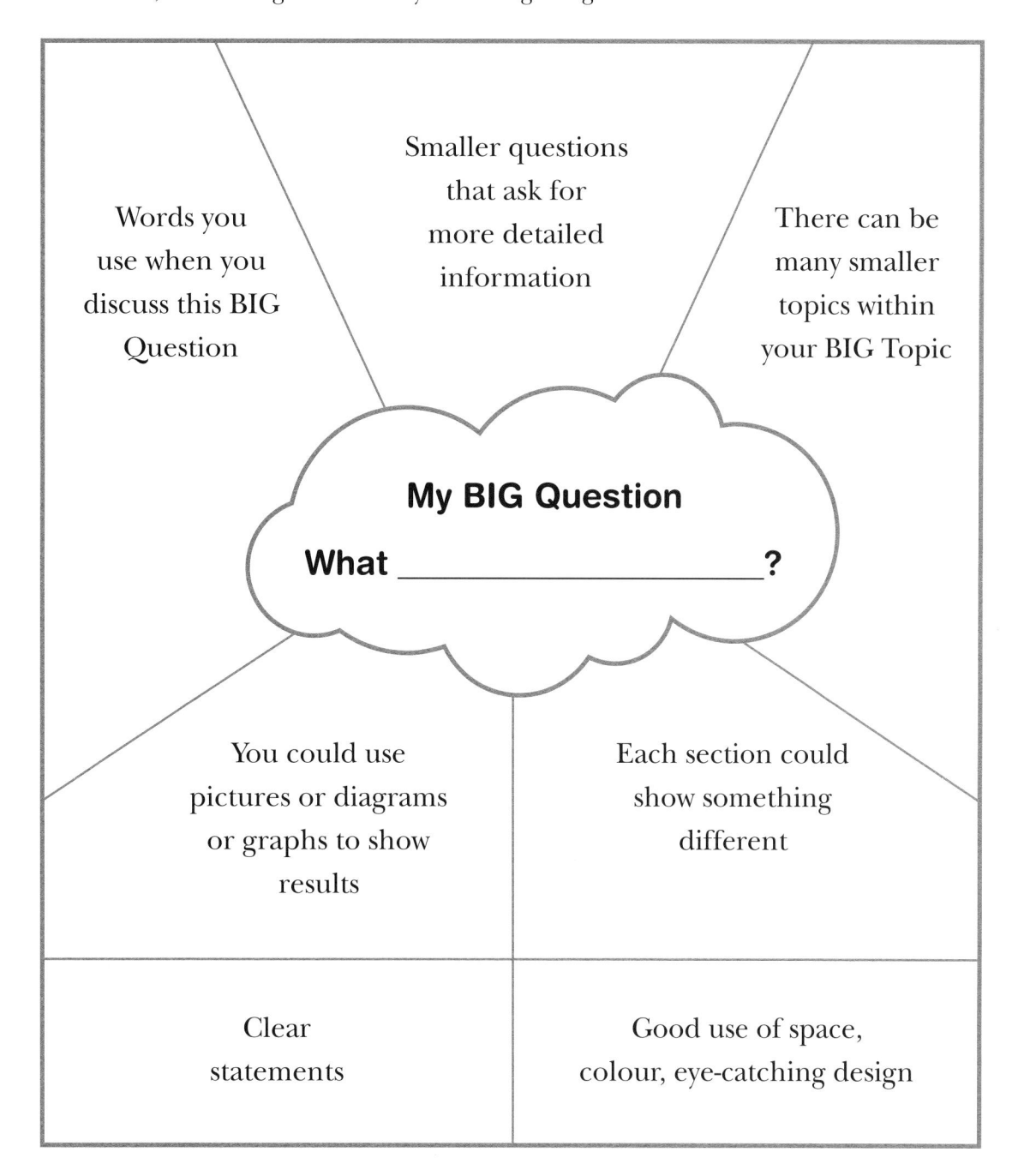

Words you use when you discuss this BIG Question	Smaller questions that ask for more detailed information	There can be many smaller topics within your BIG Topic
My BIG Question — What _____?		
You could use pictures or diagrams or graphs to show results		Each section could show something different
Clear statements		Good use of space, colour, eye-catching design

© TTS Group Ltd, 2012

Unit 2.2

Learning *Quests*   GOOD QUESTIONS TO INVESTIGATE

Pre-*Quest*: The Story So Far ...

When we are investigating something, we are often trying to solve a problem of some kind. If a lack of information is causing the problem, we must use whatever we can to make the best decision. The problem-solving process generally follows these six main steps. Place the descriptions of these steps in the shaded box below alongside the correct name of the step in the following table.

Six-step Problem-solving Process

1. Identify the problem	
2. Brainstorm possible answers	
3. Consider each of the solutions	
4. Choose one and try it out	
5. Reflection— what happened?	
6. Is it solved? *or* What now?	

- Choose which answer you think could be the best to try first.
- Look at the situation and guess what you think the problem is.
- If it is not solved, start again.
- Look at what you did and see if the problem has been solved.
- Think of all sorts of ways you might be able to solve the problem.
- Try out the solution you think will most likely solve the problem.

If you don't choose the best solution first time around, it is often a good idea to check to see that you have actually identified the problem correctly. It could be that you are not solving the real problem, but just an outcome of the problem. Example: If your sink is leaking and you get a new plug to fix the problem, it will not be fixed if the actual problem is a crack in the corner of the sink!

In-*Quest*: I Understand

Here is a problem-solving chart. And here is a problem you might encounter at school. Follow the steps through to come up with a possible solution to the problem.

Scenario: You seem to be interested in far more exciting topics than the other children in your class, but when you try to talk about your interests, they make fun of you for using big words and don't want to talk with you.
Step 1: Identify the actual problem
Step 2: Brainstorm possible answers
Step 3: Consider the merit of each of the solutions
Step 4: Choose the best solution and try it out—describe it here
Step 5: Describe what happened when you tried your solution
Step 6: Has the problem been solved?

If your problem hasn't been solved, what will you do now? _____

_____

💡 Quest–ion: What If I … ?

Is there a method you could use that would give you more confidence that the solution you choose is going to work? In the table below, give a point score out of three for each of the following factors. Two possible solutions to the scenario from the **In–Quest** on the previous page might be (1) ignore them and walk away, and (2) explain what some of your big words mean as you talk to them.

Suggested Solution	Best answer 3	Not so good 2	Worst case 1	Grand TOTAL
1st Solution: Ignore them and walk away:				
Rate these criteria: Helps to build friendships Encourages bullying Takes a long time Is upsetting to others Is helpful to others Helps you to confront issues Helps your self-esteem	*Avoids conflict*	*Shows indifference*	*Not very proactive*	
Scores				
2nd Solution: Explain some of the words:				
Rate these criteria: Helps to build friendships Encourages bullying Takes a long time Is upsetting to others Is helpful to others Helps you to confront issues Helps your self-esteem	*Shows you care*	*Encourages participation*	*Could be seen as pushy*	
Scores				

Which solution looks better when you rate the solutions this way? _____

Why? _____

Is the solution the same as the one you would have chosen by yourself? _____

Why? _____

💡 Con-*Quest*: Look What I've Done!

Here is a problem-solving chart. Think about a problem you are experiencing at school and then follow the six problem-solving steps you have learned to find the best solution you can to resolve your problem.

Rate each solution, using suitable criteria you have chosen, and then list your solutions according to their ratings. Select the highest-scoring solution to try out. If this first one doesn't solve your problem, try the second best one, and so on. Do this for a week or two to see if it helps solve the problem. If your problem still isn't solved, can you think of a way to change your solutions that might make them more successful? Test these revised solutions out for another week or two, and see if the situation gets better.

You might like to photocopy this chart and enlarge it for writing on.

A situation that I often encounter at school that I would like to solve is …
Step 1: Identify the actual problem:
Step 2: Brainstorm possible solutions:
Step 3: Consider the merit of each of the solutions: Criteria:　　　　　　　　　　　Solution 1　　Solution 2　　Solution 3   TOTALS:
Step 4: Choose the best solution and try it out. Write this solution here.
Step 5: What happened when you tried out your solution?
Step 6: Has the problem been solved?

Unit Three: Personal Space

Teacher Notes

What is personal space? For many people, it's just having enough room to move about without being disturbed by others. But some gifted children need much more space of their own than other children require. Just as a person suffering from claustrophobia needs to have more breathing room than is usual, so do some gifted children, especially those with perfectionist tendencies. Some can become so upset if they are bumped when they are working (on a drawing, perhaps) that it becomes imperative to give them a particularly wide berth, to avoid any accidents! The negative response these incidents tend to attract makes it much easier to give the children additional space in the first place. It is simply one of their learning needs that we should identify and accommodate in our classrooms.

And it is not always just physical space these children need. Some also need a considerable amount of emotional space. They need "room" to accommodate their often very different responses to a situation, and they often need a longer time than is usual to resolve matters. School norms can sometimes be so far from these children's natural ways of learning and living that they need extra time to adjust and get over any initial antagonism these can cause. We need to allow gifted pupils the freedom to be different, and not to feel condemned for being different.

Emotional space can also refer to the type of "bubble" of protection gifted children put around themselves to avoid being hurt in ways they have experienced in the past. This bubble could involve physically withdrawing from situations that have had a negative impact on them, such as those encountered on the sports field or in various social situations. Or it might mean building walls in their minds to protect themselves from outside influences and expectations. The strong will and determination these children often show when they think they are being unjustifiably reprimanded can be seen just as strongly when they decide to "turn a blind eye to something" or when they defy a teacher's directions to complete their work in a particular way.

I have found it is of little worth to try to out-argue a gifted child. The best response is to ask them and listen to their interpretation of the situation before you reach any preconception of what you think might have happened. I find this approach nearly always diverts what could become a very sticky battle of wills. In many cases, the children have such a different take on the situation that you are left wondering, "Why didn't I think of that?"

Unit 3.1

Learning *Quest*

GIVE ME SPACE

Pre-*Quest*: The Story So Far ...

There are two plan spaces below. In each, draw in blue the area of your own personal space at school and then at home. When you have done that, use a red pen or pencil to adjust the blue area to what you would prefer to have as your own space. Try to draw as accurately as possible. You might want to do your plans on separate sheets of paper.

School Classroom Floor Plan: show doors, desks, mat space, library corner, etc

Home Floor Plan: show your bedroom area and other space you occupy, either by yourself or with your family

💡 In-Quest: I Understand

Consider the following scenarios and then explain why you think the person involved might want lots of space around them.

A. Making a working model of a sailing ship out of fine balsa-wood and light cotton rigging.

B. Cooking pizzas (including chopping all the vegetables and meats, pouring sauces, and moving the food to and from the oven).

C. Practising goal-shooting at the goal-mouth on the hockey field.

D. Watching an outdoor concert on a really hot summer's day.

💡 *Quest*–ion: What If I ... ?

In the following scenarios, what could happen if you got too close to these animals?

Alligator

Stingray

Bees circling round a beehive

Cobra

Your own example:

Con-*Quest*: Look What I've Done!

I have redesigned my classroom to suit my needs better. I have labelled all the important places in the key below (adding some of my own) and made sure there is still enough room for at least 25 pupils.

Room _____ at _____ School

Key

- ☐ Whiteboard
- ☐ Teacher's desk
- ☐ Art area
- ☐ Mat space
- ☐ Library shelves
- ☐ Computer desks
- ☐ Display table
- ☐
- ☐ 25 pupil desks
- ☐ Shelves
- ☐
- ☐

Unit 3.2

Learning *Quests*

BURSTING YOUR BUBBLE

💡 Pre-*Quest*: The Story So Far ...

The new craze of **Zorb-Walking** has come to your town. This activity requires you to climb inside a thick, heavy plastic bubble, which you can walk around on the grass or in the water. It is like walking inside a spherical doughnut!

How would you feel if you were walking around inside a see-through bubble...

- on water? _____
- on grass? _____

Could you control how fast you go?

_____
_____

Would you be frightened the Zorb might burst? Why or why not?

_____
_____

How would the cushion of air between the two inside layers affect safety?

_____
_____

Could you stay inside a long time? Why or why not?

_____
_____

What would be some benefits of Zorb-Walking?

_____
_____

© TTS Group Ltd, 2012

In-Quest: I Understand

How do these products use a cushion of air or water (or something else) to work?

- Lilo/Air bed
- Water bed
- Hovercraft
- Air hockey game
- Atmosphere of the Earth
- Spacesuit
- Whales
- Fire-fighters' suits
- Wetsuits
- Thermal underclothing

Can you name some others? List them here. _____

💡 *Quest*–ion: What If I ... ?

What if I ... created my own form of "cushion" to protect myself?

_____
_____

What sorts of things would I need or want to protect myself from?

_____
_____

How could I use words to protect me?

_____
_____

Could I use "ignoring others" to protect me? Why or why not?

_____
_____

When can words feel like darts or arrows fired into us?

_____
_____

How can I deflect those arrows so that they don't hurt me?

_____
_____

What sorts of scars can damaging words cause?

_____
_____

What do you think of the saying, "Sticks and stones can break my bones, but words will never hurt me"? Is it true, or can words hurt you just as much as physical injuries? Why or why not?

_____
_____
_____

Con-*Quest*: Look What I've Done!

I've invented a "Gifted Pupil Safety Suit", and here is my drawing of it. My suit, which has its own special name (please label it on the line given), is an imaginary, protective one that makes me feel much safer and happier at school. I have added all these features to help me with things I do differently to others at school.

My _____ Suit

Unit Four:
Tenacity and Compromise

Teacher Notes

The essence of tenacity is "sticking to your guns!" Compromise, on the other hand, is the act of each person "giving a little". Teachers often complain about gifted pupils who are very stubborn; these pupils believe what they believe and there is no room for movement. I want to throw a contentious thought in here—how willing are we to compromise on our thoughts, beliefs, or ways of doing things in the classroom? If we are to teach anything, we are told it is much more likely to be learned if we model it ourselves. Food for thought?

However tenacious pupils might be in regard to subjects they are passionate about, they can also be overwhelmed by fear of failure, and unwilling to start other subjects or topics unless they are absolutely sure of success. As their mentor and guide, we need to find ways to lessen their fears by allowing them to experience failure in small steps and thereby help them build resilience into their learning journeys. A good way of doing this is to have them read and discuss stories about people in history, or familiar events they can identify with. Bibliotherapy, as it is called, is the practice of using books to help people enlarge their experiences and overcome difficulties by reading about how others have succeeded in difficult circumstances.

Younger gifted pupils often know the moral behind the stories they are told when young. They can relate to the deeper meanings and apply the situations into their own lives. They also tend to have much greater empathy than their peers for the weak and underprivileged, and a higher sensitivity toward grief and sense of loss in all sorts of tragic circumstances. The sub-units within this fourth unit ask them to discuss a well-known fable, *The Tortoise and the Hare*, and then the encouraging story of Helen Keller. The work they do in relation to these stories should encourage them to see that sticking to a goal can achieve success, even in unlikely situations.

There will be times in your dealings with gifted pupils when you feel progress is not being made. However, sticking at it, for the sake of these youngsters who need our guidance, can reap success, even if we see little, if any, evidence of it in our time with them. Helen Keller would have learned to communicate only a little in her first year of learning, and that was with her one-to-one teacher. The compromises you are able to make early in these young pupils' schooling will hopefully set them up for greater success in the future.

Unit 4.1

Learning *Quest*   THE TORTOISE AND THE HARE

💡 Pre-*Quest*: The Story So Far ...

> There once was a speedy hare who bragged about how fast he could run. Tired of hearing him boast, Slow and Steady, the tortoise, challenged him to a race. All the animals in the forest gathered to watch. Hare ran down the road for a while and then paused to rest. He looked back at Slow and Steady and cried out, "How do you expect to win this race when you are walking along at your slow, slow pace?" Hare stretched himself out alongside the road and fell asleep, thinking, "There is plenty of time to relax."
>
> Slow and Steady walked and walked. He never, ever stopped until he came to the finish line. The animals who were watching cheered so loudly for Slow and Steady that they woke up Hare. Hare stretched and yawned and began to run again, but it was too late. Slow and Stready was over the line. After that, Hare always reminded himself, "Don't brag about your lightning pace, for Slow and Steady won the race!"

What does this last line mean? "Don't brag about your lightning pace, for Slow and Steady won the race!"

_____

_____

_____

Think of another fable that teaches us about being committed to what we are doing. Ideas for stories you might consider are The Pitcher and the Crow, Mice in Council, otherwise known as Belling the Cat, or The Lion and the Mouse. Find a fable such as these ones from your library and read it. What is the moral of this story?

_____

_____

_____

In your exercise book or on the back of this sheet, draw a picture of the characters from the fable you have chosen. Show them saying an appropriate phrase in a speech bubble.

In-*Quest*: I Understand

What can I do if I don't know something?

Do I need to know about everything? Why or why not?

What is good about having to ask someone to help you? Beyond giving you the answer to your question, how can doing this help you?

How can someone asking you questions help them as well?

Apart from the library or internet, what places can you go to get information?

What is a mentor? (Look this word up in the dictionary or an encyclopaedia if you need to.)

💡 *Quest*-ion: What If I Wanted to Find out About … ?

The subject I would really like to find out more about is _____ .

- Tick the activities below that would help you learn more about your topic:

    ☐ See what I already know about the topic

    ☐ Think about questions I might like to ask

    ☐ Think about places related to my topic

    ☐ Ask someone else what they know

- What places could I visit to find out about my topic? _____
  _____

- Who could I ask about my topic? (These people don't have to be people you already know.) _____
  _____

- What if I don't understand something I hear or read? What should I do then?
  _____
  _____

- What three questions would I most like to ask about my topic?

    1. _____
    2. _____
    3. _____

What else could I do?	Where else could I go?	Who else could I ask?

You may need to ask an adult how to answer some of these questions. That is all part of "What else could I do?" So, which adults could you ask? List them in your exercise book.

Did you find out what you wanted to know? If not, what other things do you think you could do to find the information? Write them in your exercise book.

When we find out information, sometimes it gives us ideas for more questions. On the next page, write one question you still have about this topic.

Con-*Quest*: Look What I've Done!

My further research question is _____

_____

_____

This is what I have found out …

These are the names of the books I read, people I asked, and the places I visited to find out about this last question.

- _____
- _____
- _____
- _____
- _____
- _____

- _____
- _____
- _____
- _____
- _____
- _____

© TTS Group Ltd, 2012

Unit 4.2

Learning *Quests*   **HELEN KELLER**

Pre-*Quest*: The Story So Far …

> Helen Keller was an amazing person. Imagine that you couldn't see these words or hear them spoken, but that you could still talk, write, read, and make friends. In fact, you went to college, wrote nearly a dozen books, travelled all over the world, met 12 United States presidents, and lived to be 87. That was Helen Keller! She came from a small farming town in America, and she taught the whole world to respect people who are blind and deaf.
>
> Helen was born a normal baby in 1880, but less than 18 months later, after being very ill, she became both blind and deaf. For Helen, life became one of living in a whole new world with completely new rules, and she became very angry and frustrated. When she was seven, her parents hired a tutor named Anne Sullivan to help them with Helen. Anne was very strict, but she was also very determined to help Helen learn to communicate. Anne had learned to spell words with her hands, and she tried to teach Helen this skill, but Helen had become deaf so young that she didn't know what these words meant. One day at the water fountain, Anne taught Helen by making her hold one hand under the water. Then she spelled "W-A-T-E-R" into Helen's other hand. It was electric! The feeling turned into a word. Immediately, Helen bent down and tapped the ground; Anne spelled "earth". This event changed Helen's whole attitude and from there she went on learning very quickly. Helen did many wonderful things before she died in 1968.

- What was Helen Keller's "BIG Problem"?

  _____

- How did she try to resolve this problem?

  _____

- Who did she get help from?

  _____

- How did this help her?

  _____

- What might have happened if Helen had tried to learn traditional Braille to communicate with other people? (Answer in your exercise book.)

In-*Quest*: I Understand

Some people like Helen Keller have very big difficulties to overcome, and they do not get everything they try "right" first time. The greater the difficulties, the more mistakes we are likely to make. By learning from our mistakes, we can move on to new learning. What are some examples of mistakes that you could make as a child, but that you can learn from as well?

1. *Example:* If you touch something that is hot, you learn it hurts, and after a few times, you'll remember the pain you experienced previously, and you'll hesitate before touching hot things again.

2.

3.

4.

5.

6.

Quest–ion: What If I … ?

When we play games and sports, we need to realise that we may not get everything right first time. If you were playing these sports or games, what extra chances do you get in the rules to have a better turn if your first one or two turns were not so good?

Examples:

a. In **rounders**, you get three strikes at the ball before you have to run. If you don't hit the ball on the first two turns, you still have a third turn before you must try to run to first base.

In running races,

b. In **swimming**, if you dive into the water off the start, before the gun, you get one more chance to have a better start.

In tennis,

c. In **netball**, as long as you have the ball in your circle, you can have as many tries to shoot a goal as you want.

In the card game "Snap",

In cricket,

In "Scrabble",

In rugby,

In "Hangman",

Con-*Quest*: Look What I've Done!

I have invented a game (indoors or outdoors) that gives people a second chance if they don't quite get it right first time around. The game recognises we can't be perfect every time we step up to take our turn. Describe the game, its goal, and how to win (give it a name too):

List the instructions or draw the positions of players etc. at the start of the game.

1. _____
2. _____
3. _____
4. _____
5. _____

Here are the main rules of the game:

1. _____
2. _____
3. _____
4. _____
5. _____

The sorts of skills my game is trying to teach are ... _____

_____

The age group that the game most suits is ... _____

_____

Unit Five: Overcoming Frustration

Teacher Notes

Every day, scientists are learning more and more about the complexities of how our brains work. They can now watch the various sections of the brain that become active whenever we perform certain tasks. We have long known, of course, about the role of the brain. Back in the 5th century BC, Hippocrates told us that, *"Men ought to know that from the brain, and from the brain only, arise our pleasures, joys, laughters and jests, as well as our sorrows, pains, griefs and tears."* However, modern science is telling us much more about just *how* the brain operates.

In line with this work, researchers have found that we can base our learning on use of three main cues: auditory, visual, and kinaesthetic (hands on). Auditory learners gain understanding through the spoken word, which has been the basis of our education system for many years. People who prefer to learn things from pictures, diagrams, or trying things out for themselves, however, have been less well-catered for. Extremely visual learners often struggle to read once the pictures disappear from their early school readers, and in the worst cases, their dyslexia (inability to decode the written word) can hinder their learning tremendously.

My reason for having a unit on visual learning and dyslexia within a book for gifted pupils is that, quite often, dyslexia is associated with giftedness. A child may present as very verbally advanced, but fail to produce written work. The frustration caused by their inability to express themselves on paper, and their desire to avoid written work, can lead to a very difficult time for both the pupil and the teacher.

Early diagnosis and an acceptance of alternative products to the usual written assignments can greatly enhance the attitudes of a gifted child, who is also dyslexic, towards school and learning. Unfortunately, there is a fine line between recognising a learning need (often masked by the verbal intelligence of the child) and writing such children off as having a "bad attitude" and for not trying to help themselves. Accepting that the situation for these pupils is difficult, and working towards dealing with the frustration positively, is an important goal for those of you teaching these children while they are still young.

Unit 5.1

Learning *Quest*   GETTING STARTED

💡 Pre-*Quest*: The Story So Far …

News time at school—so far this probably won't have been a problem for you, because you are likely to be quite able to stand and talk about a number of topics. But now you and your classmates are getting older, the teacher wants you to write your news into your book. This is a problem for some children, for various reasons, one of which is dyslexia. Think of creative ways that you could report your news to the class that neither depends on writing lots of words nor on just doing a morning talk to the class. Write your ideas in the spaces below.

Example 1: Be news-reporters and interview one another about the latest local news.

Example 2: Make a "newsline", and peg strips of news to it like streamers (each strip should be just one or two short sentences).

Choose one of these ideas and try it out when your class is sharing news. Do this for a week or two. Think carefully about what you can do to make sure people read or take part in the news process. Write your ideas here.

_____
_____
_____
_____

© TTS Group Ltd, 2012

In-*Quest*: I Understand

There are many different ways we can show someone we understand what we have been discussing. Using the life cycle of a butterfly as an example, try out all these different ways of showing you know the four main stages of the life cycle—the egg, the caterpillar, the chrysalis and, finally, the butterfly. Do this work on separate paper or in your exercise book.

A short report ...

Use these main headings ...

Title:

Introduction:

Explanation of the individual stages of the life cycle:

Conclusion:

A labelled diagram ...

- Draw the four main stages of the life cycle and join them in a circle with arrows that show the direction in which the cycle is to be read.

- Label each stage with a name that describes that particular stage best.

- Draw a small picture that shows what the butterfly looks like at each part of the life cycle.

A drama or dance showing the passage of time

First, you must think about the main activity at each part of the life cycle. For example, at the caterpillar stage, the main activity is eating to prepare for the long time of no eating that occurs during the chrysalis stage.

Next, you must decide what sort of body movements can show this type of action best.

Put all these movements into the correct sequence and perform your drama or dance.

A chart showing the days and what happened as each day passed ...

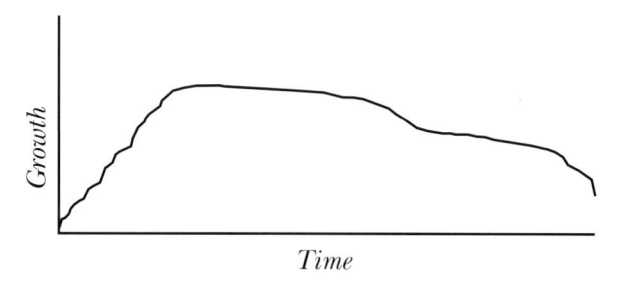

Record on a graph what happens as the time passes. You may need extra labels to describe major changes at certain times on the graph, e.g., when the chrysalis is formed.

Which did you find easier to do? _____

Why? _____

Did the audience understand this method as well? _____

Why or why not? _____

Quest–ion: What If I ... ?

How can we help pupils who have difficulties with the direction certain numbers and letters should face? Many dyslexic pupils reverse their b's and d's for example. One way to help them remember is to use the "word bed". If you look at the word, it appears to be drawn a bit like a bed, with the tall sticks of the letters forming the bed head and the bed end.

$$bed = \text{[bed drawing]}$$

Even looking at the term **b's** and **d's** shows the same bed head and end. This technique can help remind these children as they try to shape the letter in the right direction. Can you think of any other ways to help them remember the direction of these letters?

- _____
- _____
- _____

- _____
- _____
- _____

Can you think of a similar type of prompt to help children remember which way to place their **6's** and **9's** and the confusing **p's** and **q's** or to differentiate between a "**s**" and a "**z**" or a "**3**" and a "**5**"? Write or draw your ideas in the boxes.

6 and 9	p and q

s and z	3 and 5

©TTS Group Ltd, 2012

Con-*Quest*: Look What I've Done!

Create an artwork collage that is made up only of the confusing letters and numbers we have talked about in this unit. Make sure every letter or number you have used is drawn the correct way, as below.

b , d   p , q   s , z   3 , 5   6 , 9

Unit 5.2

Learning *Quests*   HIEROGLYPHICS

Pre-*Quest*: The Story So Far ...

Throughout history, people have used pictures of various sorts to communicate with one another. Early cave drawings, inscriptions on tombstones and tablets of stone, and texts on papaya are just some of the early forms of written communication used. Some cultures still use text based on pictures (such as those used by the Japanese and Chinese). Why is it that we settled on written, rather than pictographic, words and letters in the Western world?

Do you think the written method is more or less helpful than pictographic methods? Give reasons for you answer.

_____

_____

_____

_____

Is it possible that picture-based symbols are actually better than words at helping a greater number of people understand? Think about international signs for toilets, danger, airport, train, etc. Give reasons for your answer.

_____

_____

_____

_____

Choose one of the types of writing symbols mentioned above and tell us some more about it. What do you already know about when it was used? And by whom? What do some of the symbols mean?

_____

_____

_____

_____

_____

© TTS Group Ltd, 2012

💡 In-*Quest*: I Understand

Here is a simple code. Use it to decipher the question below. Answer the question using the same code. *Note:* the real alphabet is in bold letters on the top and the code is underneath.

A	**B**	**C**	**D**	**E**	**F**	**G**	**H**	**I**	**J**	**K**	**L**	**M**
Z	A	B	C	D	E	F	G	H	I	J	K	L

N	**O**	**P**	**Q**	**R**	**S**	**T**	**U**	**V**	**W**	**X**	**Y**	**Z**
M	N	O	P	Q	R	S	T	U	V	W	X	Y

Question:

VGDM CN XNT SGHMJ BNCDR RGNTKC AD TRDC ZMC VGX?

Write your answer in code here:

_____
_____
_____
_____
_____

Check your coding by deciphering your coded answer here:

_____
_____
_____
_____
_____

Write a coded question in your exercise book and give it to a friend to decipher.

Quest–ion: What If I ... ?

- What sort of code could I use on the internet to keep my work safe or away from the eyes of other people? What things would I have to consider first? (Consider, for example, what symbols you could use, and how you could share the deciphering code with only those people who you want to read it.)

_____
_____

- How easy would it be to use a picture-based code?

_____
_____

- What would be some of the problems of using a picture-based code?

_____
_____

- What are webdings? (You may need to look this up on Google first.)

_____
_____

Can you make a new simple "webding"-style alphabet that would suit young children learning to read? Create one for each of the letters of the alphabet below.

A	B	C	D	E	F	G	H	I

J	K	L	M	N	O	P	Q	R

S	T	U	V	W	X	Y	Z

© TTS Group Ltd, 2012

Con-Quest: Look What I've Done!

Your friend has created a coded language and written a coded letter to you. They also sent you the deciphering code in a separate envelope, but it got damaged in the post. Use this damaged code to decipher as many letters as you can, and then see if you can work out the full code from the remains of the damaged coding sheet. Write a reply to your friend using what you suspect is the actual code.

B	C	D	E	F	G	H
D	G	K	O	U	W	

J	K	L	M	N	O	P
Y	E	H	L	P	V	X

S	T	U	V
I	J	M	N

C Q B P J J V V F W B P C I O B I O G F O J

_ _ _ _ _ _ _ _ _ _ _ _ _ _ _ _ _ _ _ _ _ _

L O O J C P W Q Z O F O J Z O J O B L G B P X H B P

_ _ _ _ _ _ _ _ _ _ _ _ _ _ _ _ _ _ _ _ _ _ _ _ _ _

J B G J C G I U V F V M F L C K P C W Z J F B C K V P

_ _ _ _ _ _ _ _ _ _ _ _ _ _ _ _ _ _ _ _ _ _ _ _ _ _ _

J Z O X B P J F S! Q Z B J P C W Z J K V S V M

_ _ _ _ _ _ _ _ _ _! _ _ _ _ _ _ _ _ _ _ _ _ _ _

I M W W O I J?

_ _ _ _ _ _ _?

Could you answer their question in code too? _____.

52   ©TTS Group Ltd, 2012

Suggested Answers for Specified Activities

Unit One: A Community of Learners

1.1 Working as a Community

- **Pre-*Quest*: The Story So Far… (page 9)**

    The important point here is to make pupils aware that once they have called out an answer it robs everyone else in the room of the opportunity to think of an answer for themselves. The chance can't be given back to them. It has gone as soon as the answer is shouted out (presuming of course they have the correct answer!).

- **In-*Quest*: I Understand (page 10)**
    - Older people may not appreciate tongue and other body-part piercings the same way younger generations do.
    - Lock and put grills on doors and windows.
    - The need to turn toward Mecca and pray throughout the day; eating some meat.
    - Some cultures say they will do something "just now" but actually mean they will do it later!
    - It is the responsibility of both the speaker and the listener to make sure the communication is received and understood.

Unit 1.2 The Ants and the Bees

- **In-*Quest*: I Understand (page 14)**

    Workers: These are the labourers, machine operators, computer operators, etc.

    Builders: These are the skilled tradespeople.

    Caretakers: These are the service workers who maintain the buildings, machines, etc.

    Designers: These are the creative members of the community—the ideas people, thinkers and problem-solvers.

    Leaders: These people have the oversight of the community. They are ultimately responsible for their community's well-being. Other jobs could be transporter, communicator, educator, etc.

Unit Two: So Many Questions

Unit 2.2 Good Questions to Investigate

- **In-*Quest*: I Understand (page 23)**

    Some ideas for answers to these questions might be:

    Step 1—the actual problem could be that they feel threatened by the big words you use, because they are embarrassed to let you know they don't understand.

    Step 2—brainstorm possible solutions; explain your big words more; make them feel free to ask questions; use words they are familiar with.

    Step 3—explanations will help them understand and learn new words as well. If they feel they can ask questions they may be more willing to listen; sometimes there will be words or terms they are just not going to know.

    Step 4—choose the best solution; what this is will depend on the class. Maybe using the words but explaining them simply as you go will work best.

    Step 5—what happened? Did you still get laughed at, or were some more interested this time? It may be you have to try it a few times before you can answer this accurately.

Step 6—problem solved, or you may need to go back to a second try that offers a different solution. If none of your ideas works, you may need to determine if you have identified the problem accurately in the first place

- *Quest*-ion: What If I … ? (page 24)

Protecting oneself from lack of kindness from others is an important and necessary goal for some gifted pupils. They are not always easily accepted into their peer groups and can find schooling a lonely experience if they don't receive caring and understanding adult support.

Unit Three: Personal Space

Unit 3.1 Give Me Space

- **In–*Quest*: I Understand (page 28)**

    a. Balsa is very breakable, and the cotton rigging could get easily tangled.

    b. Hot ovens can burn; sharp knives can cut. Would not want to be accidentally bumped!

    c. Hockey stick and ball can injure if you are too close; practising shooting goals is an important part of the game, so concentration is needed.

    d. In the heat of the day, it would not be very comfortable to have sweaty people too close. Need some room to relax and allow the fresh air to circulate.

Unit Four: Tenacity and Compromise

Unit 4.1 The Tortoise and the Hare

- **Pre–*Quest*: The Story So Far… (page 36)**

    The Pitcher and the Crow: The crow was committed to getting a drink, and so continued to fill the jug with pebbles until the water level rose high enough for him to drink the water from the spout.

    Mice in Council, otherwise known as **Belling the Cat:** The mice were committed to finding a solution to the problem of the cat creeping up on them and putting them in danger of losing their lives. A pity their commitment to finding a solution didn't go as far as finding a "workable" solution.

    The Lion and the Mouse: The mouse was committed to helping the lion after he had himself been spared his life. Despite the lion thinking the mouse would be of no use to him, he was shown how the mouse's perseverance at the job of nibbling through the ropes eventually freed the lion.

- **In–*Quest*: I Understand (page 37)**

    Apart from the obvious answers, don't forget they can also seek information from local council, their local MP or the Prime Minister's Office, and from the public relations officers at large companies.

- **Con–*Quest*: Look What I've Done! (page 39)**

    This activity offers the very earliest recognition that work done by others is valued and that we can't just copy it and call it our own. We must acknowledge the people whose work has helped us find the answers to our questions.

Unit 4.2: Helen Keller

- **Pre–*Quest*: The Story So Far … (page 40)**

    a. Helen wasn't born blind and deaf, but she developed both of these difficulties after she had a very bad illness when she was less than two years old. Because of her age, she could not just learn ordinary Braille, because she didn't know what the words meant, as she had been very young when she could see and hear.

    b. Helen got a tutor when she was seven, and this person helped her to learn a way to match words with things she could feel.

    c. This tutor was Anne Sullivan.

    d. Helen started to experience things and find out names for them and this made her want to learn more and more.

e. Helen had become very angry with life. If she hadn't changed her attitude when she was seven, she would never have been able to learn and communicate so much with other people. She ended up helping other disabled people like herself by writing books about her experiences.

- **In–*Quest*: I Understand (page 41)**

Some examples might be:

- If you get a bee or a wasp sting, you learn to be more careful near them in future.
- If you fall off your bike or your skateboard, you will learn to take more care next time.
- If you touch electrical cords with wet hands, you could get a shock that will remind you to be careful.
- If you push a swing, you might quickly learn that it comes back to hit you.

- ***Quest*–ion: What If I … ? (page 42)**

In cricket, you don't have to run each time you hit the ball, only when you think you have hit it far enough to get in a complete run.

In rugby, you can keeping throwing the ball to another player in your team if you get tackled, as long as you don't pass it forward and you keep it in your possession.

In running races, you have the same false start procedure as in swimming—one chance to break, and then it must be a good start or you are disqualified.

In tennis, you get two chances to serve the ball into the correct square on the opponent's side. Occasionally, if you hit the net, you get another second chance as well.

In the card game "Snap", you can say "Snap" without penalty, but if you are to win the round, you must be the first one to say "Snap".

In "Scrabble", you can make up words of any length, and this also means you can add to ones already there. If you haven't got any good letters left, you are allowed to swap them with some of the remaining letters.

In "Hangman", you can guess letters for as long as you still have parts to draw on your hangman.

Unit Five: Overcoming Frustration

Unit 5.2 Hieroglyphics

- **In–*Quest*: I Understand (page 50)**

Question translates to: When do you think codes should be used and why?

Answer: Among possible answers are keeping secrets safe, sending damaging messages, stimulating the brain into thinking, and for fun.

- ***Quest*–ion: What If I … ? (page 51)**

Picture-based codes can be written into computer code, but they cannot always stand for every word we might need. Limited amounts can be stored on the keyboard.

Webdings belong to a computerised font that shows little pictures of common items, as below:

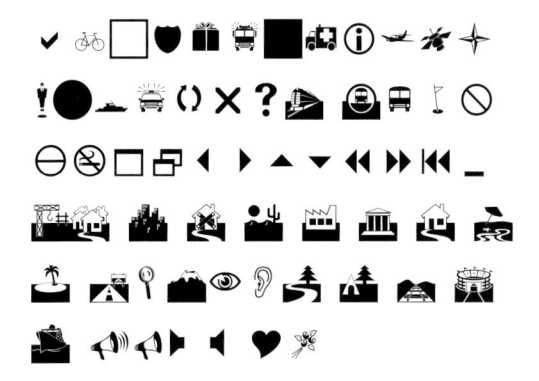

- **Con–*Quest*: Look What I've Done! (page 52)**

The coded question reads, "I want to organise a secret meeting where the team can plan tactics for our midnight raid on the pantry! What night do you suggest?"

The complete code is:

A	B	C	D	E	F	G	H	I
B	D	G	K	O	U	W	Z	C

J	K	L	M	N	O	P	Q	R
Y	E	H	L	P	V	X	A	F

S	T	U	V	W	X	Y	Z
I	J	M	N	Q	R	S	T

© TTS Group Ltd, 2012